Brain Building

Develop Your Logic Muscles

Karl Albrecht

© 1984 – 2012 Karl Albrecht

THE AUTHOR:

Dr. Karl Albrecht is an executive management consultant, lecturer, and author of more than 20 books on professional achievement, organizational performance, and business strategy.

He is a recognized authority on cognitive styles and the development of advanced thinking skills. His books *Social Intelligence: The New Science of Success*, *Practical Intelligence: The Art and Science of Common Sense*, and his *Mindex Thinking Style Profile* are used in business and education.

The Mensa society presented him with its lifetime achievement award, for significant contributions by a member to the understanding of intelligence. Originally a physicist, and having served as a military intelligence officer and business executive, he now consults, lectures, and writes about whatever he thinks would be fun.

Thoughts on Thinking . . .

"Five percent of people think. Another ten percent think they think. And the other 85 percent would sooner die than think."

~ Thomas Edison, American inventor

"If we once start thinking, no one can guarantee where we shall come out – except to say that many ends, objects, and institutions are doomed. Every thinker puts some portion of an apparently stable world in peril, and no one can wholly predict what will emerge in its place."

~ John Dewey, American educator

"Who can say which will be more important in the end – landing on the moon, or understanding the human mind?"

~ Tenzin Gyatso (14th Dalai Lama)

CONTENTS

11
PUTTING IT TOGETHER *87*

PREFACE

Think back to a recent occasion when you had to make a decision or solve some problem that called for careful thought. Think of a time when your logical processes were really clicking well, and you came up with a really good solution. You overcame a confused situation and you put things right.

If you're like most people, you got a miniature emotional *charge* out of that experience—you had a momentary feeling of being high, potent, and effective. It felt good to be able to conquer a problem with clear, logical thought.

Like most people, you'd like to feel that way more often, on a more consistent basis. This book can help you feel that way, by helping you learn certain key thought habits and mental *tactics* that make your logical processes more powerful and reliable.

Research into the practical aspects of human thought has identified the differences between people who can think clearly and logically and people who are intimidated by it. Aside from any differences in so-called "intelligence" that may or may not exist, clear thinkers have somehow mastered certain relatively simple mental procedures that make the difference. Many skilled thinkers can't explain clearly how they go about dealing with complicated situations or intricate problems, but a careful analysis of their comments reveals a very orderly thought process at work. My research into practical thinking processes, tested and refined through a number of years of conducting the Brainpower seminar for business organizations and teaching thinking courses at an extension of the University of California, has isolated these key mental tactics and organized them into a teachable form. By understanding them and using them deliberately in various everyday situations, you can become "smarter," in a practical sense.

In this book, I will guide you on a fascinating journey—inside the human mind, where we will "listen in" on the thoughts of a person who has developed the skills of clear, logical thinking. By figuratively listening to this person think through a series of logical problems, you will see these key mental tactics in action. You will see how it is possible to organize information so effectively that you get rid of that apprehensive feeling of being overwhelmed by the problem and develop a sense of mastery over it. Then, once you have had a chance to see these thinking processes in action, you can put them to use as you work out a number of similar problems on your own. You will soon see how these mental tactics can apply in all areas of practical living and working, and you will begin using them in those situations as well.

This is *not* a book of "puzzles" in the usual sense. Rather, it is a book of guided mental exercises, using easy thinking problems for practice and skill building. I have selected each of the problems for its skill-building value rather than for its potential for frustrating or defeating you. These problems are not "tricky" in the sense that I am trying to present you with something you can't solve. There are enough "puzzle" books already, with titles that emphasize mental torture, frustration, and aggravation. I have included each of the selected problems for its ability to enlighten, rather than to exasperate. Puzzle fans may find them interesting as well, but my purpose is to teach rather than to test.

If you are one of the many people who have suffered for years from a lack of confidence in your logical faculties, and therefore steered shy of situations that would put them to the test, this book may have special value to you. It will help you see that clear, logical thinking is not a magical process or a matter of genetic endowment, but rather a process of organizing and manipulating information which you can learn. By carefully studying the basic mental procedures or tactics presented here, and by making a deliberate effort to use them in as many situations as possible, you will probably see a marked improvement in your logical skills. You will probably feel much more effective in most situations as a result.

1

INTRODUCTION

Logical thinking is simply a matter of organizing and manipulating information. Problems or situations that involve logical thinking call for structure, for relationships between facts, and for chains of reasoning that "make sense." When faced with a problem or decision that requires some kind of logical analysis, how do you react? To what extent do you think of yourself as a logical person?

Research into practical thinking processes has shown that there are two contrasting types of reactions that many people have, with relatively few folks falling in the middle. On the one hand, there is the *challenge* reaction. One person sees the situation as an opportunity for a bit of mental exercise, in addition to a problem in need of resolution. Just as a person who enjoys playing tennis responds positively to being handed a tennis racquet, so a person who enjoys clear, logical thought responds positively to being handed a situation that calls for analysis.

At the other extreme, there is the *avoidance* reaction. This person sees the situation as threatening, uncomfortable, and involving an unpleasant and defeating experience. He or she experiences what might be called the *failure reflex*, a snap-reaction feeling of dread, which originates in ancient experiences of having been defeated by situations similar to the one presenting itself. Just as the person who is in very poor physical condition tends to get negative feelings at the prospect of playing a round of tennis, so the person who has trouble with logical thinking tends to shudder at the anticipation of a round of logical thought.

Why the difference? Why is it that some people are skilled at logical thinking and enjoy it so much, while others nearly break out in hives at the mere prospect? Why have some people imprisoned themselves within a self-definition as basically scatter-brained, using the disclaimer "I'm basically intuitive" as a cop-out? Why shouldn't they be able to use their intuitive processes together with their logical processes, rather than instead of them?

The answer, for the most part, is fairly simple: experience. By various means, the logical thinker has had opportunities to master certain basic mental procedures that work well in a broad variety of situations, and has been rewarded in different ways for using these mental processes successfully. The person with an aversion to logical thinking has found this kind of experience consistently unsuccessful, defeating, and unpleasant. Because no one will repeatedly seek out experiences that threaten his or her self-esteem, this person falls into a self-reinforcing pattern of avoiding experiences that would help to develop these skills.

This explains why so many adults suffer from mathephobia in varying degrees. Learning mathematics is a highly sequential process. If you don't fully grasp a certain concept, fact, or procedure, you can never hope to grasp others that come later, which depend upon it. For example, to understand fractions you must first understand division. To understand simple equations in algebra requires that you understand fractions. Solving "word problems" depends on knowing how to set up and manipulate equations, and so on. A person who has trouble with mathematics as an adult must have been, at one time, a child who understood everything that had been presented up to that point.

But sooner or later, the child stumbled over some concept that didn't make sense. This created a blank spot in his or her learning, and as a result certain concepts that came thereafter never quite made sense either. As the child's confusion increased and feelings of inadequacy set in, he or she sooner or later concluded "I'm no good at math." For all practical purposes, this was the end of the learning process. Many people, during their adolescent years, give up on math in this way, and extend their aversive feelings to just about all situations involving the intricate mental processes of logic, sequential thinking, and organizing information. Mathephobia is a *learned* mental process, just as logical thinking is a learned mental process.

If you suffer from some degree of mathephobia, or from the more general problem of "logicophobia," you can begin to erase this self-defeating reaction in two ways. First, stop avoiding or copping out of problem-solving situations that call for logical thinking. Facing up to an uncomfortable situation, and being determined not to feel worthless if you can't solve it, goes a long way to eliminating the failure reflex. Second, you can study the specific mental techniques used by effective problem solvers, master them, and put them to use on a daily basis in a wide range of experiences. The first of these options is your responsibility. This book can help you with the second.

People with logicophobia seem to think the effective problem solver simply looks at a situation, and by some magical act just *solves* it. They don't quite realize that the logical thinker has certain fairly specific procedures at his or her disposal, which have the effect of organizing the information, reducing ambiguity, eliminating extraneous factors, zeroing in on key variables and relationships, and extracting certain findings. This is not done in one fell swoop. It is a succession of mental actions—a *sequence* of individual steps that leads to a solution, not a giant leap.

It has been proven that specific training in logical thinking processes can make people "smarter." Professors in the physics department at the University of Massachusetts created a tutorial program for physics students who were having trouble with their courses. The most common complaint these students registered was "I can do the math okay, but I have a lot of trouble with the word problems." From this, the professors concluded that the problem students were deficient in a key mental skill they called *sequential thought*. This type of thought is the ability to take a poorly organized statement of a situation and arrange it in the form of a sequential chain of statements and mathematical operations that will produce the solution. By studying the comments these students made as they attempted to solve physics problems, and by studying the comments made by graduate students who were expert problem solvers, researchers were able to develop teaching techniques to help students increase their skills at sequential thought.

In a similar vein, I have been analyzing both logical and creative thinking processes as part of my research for courses in thinking at the University of California extension, and for "Brain Power" seminars in corporations. I have found that being able to apply a simple label to a certain thought process equips a person to develop it and to put it to use on a consistent basis. The more you think about thinking, the more clearly you learn to think.

2

LET'S TAKE A
MENTAL JOURNEY

Come along with me for the next few minutes on an unusual excursion—inside the human mind. Let's listen in on the thought processes of a person who is a clear, logical thinker. We don't know who it is, man or woman, old or young, well schooled or not. We can just hear the thoughts being expressed as they move along. This person is working through one of those little thinking puzzles that require a logical attack. As you read the transcript of the person's thought processes, the symbol(!) will alert you to a *mental procedure* he or she is using to gain control over the information and organize it in such a way as to make the solution easier to grasp. Let's go.

PROBLEM

If three days ago was the day before Friday, what will the day after tomorrow be?

What's Going on
in the Thinker's Mind?

"Let's see, now . . . if three . . . hmm . . . (!)the goal is to find out what the day after tomorrow will be—right? . . . Yeah . . . It's worded a little confusingly; wonder if I can (!)rephrase it to make it easier ... Well, I can (!)reduce it to some extent; the day before Friday means Thursday, so three days ago was Thursday. ... Now, I can (!)count forward in steps to figure out what today is. So, it goes Thursday (three days ago), Friday, Saturday, and today must be Sunday. That (!)narrows it down to finding out what the day after tomorrow means. If this is Sunday, then tomorrow is Monday, and the day after tomorrow is Tuesday. So the solution is "Tuesday." Let me (!)verify that ... (counting on fingers) Thursday, Friday, Saturday, today is Sunday, then comes Monday, and finally Tuesday. Yep, it checks out. I'm hungry—guess I'll go have some lunch."

If you followed my editorial signals while listening to the flow of thoughts, you may have noticed that all of the key steps contributed to one basic purpose: organizing the available information into a useful form and progressively reducing the problem by extracting useful conclusions from what was known so far. This is basically all there is to clear, logical thought—getting the information under control and then using it.

By studying the thought processes of clear thinkers and by analyzing a variety of logical problems and situations, I have succeeded in isolating seven critical procedures that seem to spell the difference between fuzzy thinking and clear thinking. These seven mental tactics give a person a measure of control over the information in a situation, and make it easier to find solutions. I have given them simple descriptive names to make them easy to learn and memorize. Throughout this book, I will be showing you how these logical tactics work, illustrating ways to use them, and giving you opportunities to practice with them.

The seven basic logical tactics used by effective thinkers are as follows:

1. *Stepping*—attacking a problem in simple steps or stages; dividing the problem up into manageable parts; patiently exploring one thing

at a time until you can come up with a logical *chain* of facts and conclusions that give you the answer you need; drawing simple *if-then* conclusions.

2. *Picturing*—drawing a sketch, diagram, illustration, or other visual analogy you can work with.

3. *Rephrasing*—stating the problem in a different way by using terms that are more convenient for your own understanding.

4. *Fencing*—reducing the problem to a smaller scale by making certain simplifying conclusions or throwing out irrelevant considerations; putting a figurative "fence" around it to make it more manageable.

5. *Itemizing*—simply listing all of the known options, possibilities, situations, arrangements, or combinations that you need to evaluate in finding the solution.

6. *Chaining*—arranging a variety of options and suboptions in the form of a logical chain, a time sequence, or a branching tree-type diagram so you can track down and account for all of the known approaches that look feasible.

7. *Jumping the track*—stopping to reconsider the whole course of your attack on the problem; starting again with a completely different approach or a different point of view; enlarging the range of options to include unusual or novel ones, sometimes by means of a creative leap.

As you read through this book, I will show you how a skilled thinker uses each of these seven logical tactics to overcome problems that look confusing and intimidating at the start. By listening in on this person's thoughts, you will have the benefit of a role model for thinking. Each of the seven tactics is treated in a separate chapter. In each of these chapters, I will first show you several simple puzzle problems, give you a chance to work on them, and then take you on an excursion inside the mind of our expert thinker to see and hear how he or she attacks it. Then, I will offer several easy practice problems you can use for skill building. By observing a role model who uses the techniques, and then trying them on your own, you will soon become familiar with them and more comfortable in using them.

OVERCOMING
LOGICOPHOBIA

Before we study each of the seven key mental tactics in detail in the next chapters, we need to consider one very important issue. This is the issue of your *psychological reaction* to a logical challenge. As I mentioned previously, people vary widely in the extent to which they feel comfortable and confident in dealing with complex, intricate, or confused situations. Some people, usually by virtue of their early life experiences and formal education, develop a fair degree of skill in logical thinking. Others, unfortunately, again because of their particular experiences and education, develop a very strong aversion toward anything that smacks of logical analysis or logical relationships. Most people are somewhere in the middle, neither extremely good at logic, nor extremely poor. Nevertheless, many people do report feeling slightly discouraged and mildly anxious when confronted with situations that demand a logical attack. So if you consider yourself somewhat *logicophobic*, you are in good company. Probably the vast majority of people share this problem.

Logicophobia is not a terminal illness, and it can indeed be cured. You may have no desire to compete with the best scientific minds, but you probably recognize that you could benefit to some degree by increasing your mastery over basic logical processes. Here are some suggestions for anyone who wants to become more comfortable with logical thinking.

First, make up your mind to stop fighting logical thinking, and join it. By this, I mean that your own feelings of distaste for logical processes may be getting in the way of your skill because you may be deliberately avoiding situations or problems that call for logical thought. Consider the possibility that you can just deliberately change your attitude—you can *decide* to feel relaxed and at ease with these situations, whether you can solve them or not. The next time you find yourself in a logic situation, move toward it rather than away from it. Get involved with it to some extent and do as much as you can. If you're working with other people, don't let them monopolize the project simply because they may be good at logical thinking. Contribute your part and don't feel guilty about not knowing the whole answer. While you're at it, consider asking them to explain things to you, coach you, and help you develop your skills.

The second thing you can do to overcome logicophobia is to learn and apply the specific logical tactics covered in this book. Memorize the names of all seven of them and be able to define them in your own words, even if you may not feel entirely secure about using all of them. Work through every single exercise as well as you can, each time developing more and more of a feel for the processes of organized, sequential thought.

Another thing you can do to help yourself is to pay more attention to the way you talk. People who are extreme logicophobes, bordering on the scatterbrained, tend to talk in a scattered way. They jump around from one idea to another, and they neglect to tie their ideas together so other people can understand them. If you train yourself to *talk logically*, you will begin to *think* more logically. Form the habit of explaining things to people in complete sentences, using an *"A-B-C" sequence* of ideas rather than a random *"brain dump."* Train yourself to stick to one topic at a time in a discussion, and make sure you have explored it properly before you move on to the next logically related topic.

Work on developing a sense of determination in yourself about dealing with logical situations. Develop an aggressive, energetic attitude, with the feeling that you're going to attack the problem vigorously, and you don't care about the fact that you might not be able to solve it completely. You're going to give it your best shot and accomplish as much as you can.

This sense of determination will help you to deal with the *blank wall effect* so commonly found in dealing with complicated situations. By this, I mean that momentary hopeless, somewhat overwhelmed feeling you sometimes get when confronted by a problem that looms large and complex, especially if you don't immediately see an obvious starting point. Sometimes you just draw a blank, and look at the problem with no glimmer of enlightenment. You feel overwhelmed by the whole and unable to deal with its parts.

The way to cope with the blank wall effect is to simply start somewhere—by choosing some particular factor and examining it. To mix metaphors a bit, forget about the forest for a while and start looking at some of the trees. Logical problem solving is not a purely mechanical process, with all of the steps clearly laid out and executed. Every problem requires at least a certain amount of *"intelligent groping,"* in order for you to get enough of a feel for what it is all about. Once you mentally get involved with the problem, you will usually see certain lines of attack that look more fruitful than others. Teach yourself to jump in with a bit of intellectual bravado, confident that a little familiarity with the nature of the problem and its key features will enable you to decide which of the key logical tools to apply.

THINKING IN STEPS

The basis of all logical thinking is *sequential thought*. This process involves taking the important ideas, facts, and conclusions involved in a problem and arranging them in a chain-like progression that takes on a meaning in and of itself. To think logically is to think in steps. People who have difficulty with logical thinking usually have very little patience with these intricate, step-wise processes. This is especially true for those who consider themselves highly intuitive, for example, and who shudder at the mere idea of having to balance a checkbook or write out a plan for some project.

If you feel you need to improve your logical skills, the best place to start is in improving your ability to handle sequential thinking processes. You must not only learn to *tolerate* the process of thinking in deliberate, discrete steps, but you must actually develop a certain *preference* for it. Sequential thinking should be a first resort in those situations that call for it, not a last resort. There are times when an intuitive, flashtype thought process is called for, and other times when a carefully reasoned, linear process is necessary. The mentally versatile person is the one who can do both, and who feels equally comfortable with these two valuable kinds of thinking processes.

In this chapter, I will show you how you can increase your skills in sequential thinking. We will go through a series of thinking exercises, all of which require you to put your ideas into carefully constructed sequences, or progressions of thought. The more of these exercises you perform, the more you will find yourself becoming comfortable with step-wise thinking. Ready? Here we go.

I want you to figure out the ten-letter name of a famous person by constructing the name letter by letter, according to a sequence of clues. Write the individual letters of the name beside the following ten numbers, so as to form a column of letters that spell the name from top to bottom. Work with a pencil, not a pen. As you do this, pay close attention to how this process *feels* to you. Get familiar and intimate with your brain's sequential thought processes, and begin to value and enjoy them.

Practice Problem 4-1 (Stepping)

Letters of the Name

1.
2.
3.
4.
5.
6.
7.
8.
9.
10.

Here are the clues you need to deduce the name of the famous person.

1. Letters 1, 2, 3, and 4 mean "to clean."
2. Letters 3, 4, 5, and 6 are a part of the body.

3. Letters 1, 5, 6, and 7 are found on a bird.

4. Letters 8, 9, and 10 are a unit of measurement.

What is the 10-letter name of this famous person?

You probably found this exercise fairly easy. If you were careful to check what you were doing at each step, and you avoided the temptation to jump to conclusions, you probably wound up with the solution: Washington. Did you check all four of the specifications to make sure you had the right answer? This is a very important part of logical thinking—double-checking and assuring that you have put the elements of information together in a reliable way.

Well, so much for your first exercise in sequential thought, or *stepping*, as we will call it here. Now let's try some more exercises. For the next round, let's use a very interesting kind of puzzle called a *word ladder*. A word ladder is simply a series of words, in which each successive word is constructed by changing only one letter in the preceding word, keeping the arrangement of the letters exactly the same. Here is a classic example, in which we transform the word *lose* into the word *find*, by shifting one letter at a time.

EXAMPLE PROBLEM 4-1 (STEPPING)

LOSE
LONE
LINE
FINE
FIND

Get the idea? It's fairly simple and it provides an excellent form of exercise in step-wise thinking. While this exercise may be a little too elementary for the veteran puzzle fan, it is ideal for the person who needs to develop sequential thinking skills.

Now, you try it. Here are some pairs of words for you to practice on. In each case, approach the problem systematically, keeping your work organized and easy to follow. Don't be reluctant to use paper extravagantly; it's important to get the problem down clearly and understandably. Use a clean sheet of paper for each problem, and give yourself plenty of room to work. Check the solutions given at the end of the chapter only after you've given each of them a good try.

Practice Problem 4-2 (Stepping)

1. Change EAST to WEST
2. Change HEAT to COLD
3. Change LION to BEAR
4. Change HATE to LOVE

You probably found that a little concentration and patience took you a long way. If you've previously had difficulty with sequential thinking, you're probably getting more and more comfortable with it.

Now, let's move onto some other forms of step-wise thinking, this time slightly more demanding. We're going to do some "alphabet" arithmetic. In the following addition problem, each digit has been replaced by a letter of the alphabet. Any one letter always represents the same number whenever it appears. By using your logic, and applying the principles of addition, can you determine what the original numbers were? Try to work it out yourself before you read the expert thinker's version.

EXAMPLE PROBLEM 4-2 (STEPPING)

$$\begin{array}{r} Y \\ Y \\ +Y \\ \hline BY \end{array}$$

Did you work it out all right? In any case, let's review the expert thinker's internal monologue.

"Let me see . . . (!)Y plus Y plus Y equals a two-digit number (rephrasing). First, I'll try to figure out what Y is—or, on the other hand, what Y is *not*. Because 3 times Y is more than 9, *i.e.* a two-digit number, then (!)Y has to be higher than 3 (logical conclusion). Now I notice that the last digit of the answer is the same as each of the three numbers being added up. I can check by multiplication to see which numbers can give that result . . . let's see (!)only the number 5 meets that condition (fencing). Three times 5 equals 15, so Y must be 5 and B must be 1. Got it!"

Notice how the *if-then reasoning* process goes along in the expert thinker's mind. He or she takes a fact which is given, and makes a logical conclusion based upon that fact. This then becomes the basis for other conclusions, until he or she arrives at the ultimate answer.

Let's try another, similar problem.

EXAMPLE PROBLEM 4-3 (STEPPING)

$$\begin{array}{r} AB \\ +B \\ \hline BA \end{array}$$

Once again, try to work it out before reading the solution.

Ready for the solution? Here goes.

"Let me see ... it's kind of simple—only two digits to work with. Do I have enough information to solve it? Well ... (!)I'll look at the 'carry' part of the sum, and see if it tells me anything (look at 'trees'). The first digit of the answer is different from the first digit of the top number, so (!)that tells me that adding B and B produced a 'carry' (logical conclusion). That means that B has to be 5 or higher, and it can't be 5 because that would make A equal to zero, which can't be true because A is the first digit of the top number. So I've narrowed it down a bit ... let me see ... I know now that A can only be a 6, a 7, an 8, or a 9—one of those.

"Can I (!)check all four of those numbers to see what happens (try all possibilities)? Let me see ... if B equals 6, then B plus B equals 12, so A would be 2; does that work? No, because the problem would be '26 plus 6 equals 62,' which is incorrect. Then, let me try 'B equals 7.' This would give me 7 plus 7, or 14; if B equals 7, then A equals 4, so the problem would be '47 plus 7 equals 74,' which is also wrong. So B can't be 7. Let me (!)try the next one—'B equals 8' (persistence). Eight plus 8 gives 16, so it would be '68 plus 8 equals 86'— nope, wrong again. Well, 9 is the only remaining choice for B. Let me (!)check to make sure (double-checking). If B equals 9, I have 9 plus 9 equals 18, which makes A equal to 8. So the problem becomes '89 plus 9 equals 98.' That's correct. So the answer is 'A equals 8 and B equals 9.' Wish I had tried 9 first, but that's life."

Get the idea? Again, you needn't feel discouraged if you didn't get this one exactly, so long as you can follow the form of the logical attack made by the thinker. Once you've read a certain number of these kinds of examples and tried your hand at them, you'll find it starts to soak into your brain more and more.

Now, here are some alphabet-math problems for you to practice on. Keep the following points in mind as you go

1. Make sure you are physically relaxed as you approach each one.
2. Focus your concentration and don't let that apprehensive feeling set in. Approach the problem confidently and matter-of-factly, and don't worry about not getting the answer. Concentrate on going through the logical steps to get the solution.
3. Don't hesitate to use a little trial and error as you go; make a preliminary guess and check to see if it will work. You can always back up and start again.
4. Use a clean sheet of paper for each problem.
5. The letter-number assignments are different for each of the problems.

You'll find *solutions* for each at the end of the chapter.

Practice Problem 4-3 (Stepping)

$$
\begin{array}{r}
AB \\
AB \\
+AB \\
\hline
CAB
\end{array}
$$
(Hint: B can only be a _____?)

Practice Problem 4-4 (Stepping)

$$
\begin{array}{r}
ABA \\
-CA \\
\hline
AB
\end{array}
$$

I hope you found these exercises fairly easy, although some of them may have taken you a little time. I also hope you're becoming more comfortable with the technique of stepping, and that you're more aware of the value of proceeding in small, measured steps in many problem-solving situations. Train yourself to recognize the need for a step-wise attack as you confront problems that are broader and more practical in their nature. What works for these little thinking puzzles can work equally as well for larger problems involving work, dealings with other people, or the practical business of living.

Solutions to Problems

Practice Problem 4-2 (Stepping)
1. EAST, LAST, LEST, WEST.
2. HEAT, HEAD, HELD, HOLD, COLD.
3. LION, LOON, LOAN, LEAN, BEAN, BEAR.
4. HATE, LATE, LANE, LONE, LOVE.

Practice Problem 4-3 (Stepping)

```
  AB      50
  AB      50
 +AB     +50
 ───     ───
 CAB     150
```

Practice Problem 4-4 (Stepping)

```
 ABA     101
 −CA     −91
 ───     ───
  AB      10
```

5

DRAWING PICTURES

The most useful weapon you have for attacking just about any kind of a problem is a pen or a pencil. By *drawing a picture*, a sketch, a diagram, or some kind of visual representation of the problem, you immediately force it to hold still. You gain a certain degree of mastery over it.

This one factor is probably the most important difference between people who think clearly and logically and those who do not. The skilled logical thinker realizes the value of conceptualizing the problem graphically, putting the various factors down on paper, and organizing what he or she knows so far. The unskilled or inefficient thinker tends to simply sit and muse, without embarking on any particular course of mental action, as if waiting for some inspiration to strike. I call this the syndrome of *waiting for the cosmic ray*. Many unskilled thinkers seem to believe that logical thinkers simply "get" the solution to a problem in a flash—that it somehow pops into their heads fully formed. They have no idea that the logical thinker actually moves into the problem in small, clearly defined steps and develops an organized picture of it.

Very few logical problem solvers neglect the tremendous benefits of pen and paper. The skilled thinker can seldom be found without a pen somewhere on his or her person. Conversely, the fuzzy-thinking person seldom has a very high regard for those two useful implements. He or she will often encounter

situations where a pen is needed and will simply shrug help-
lessly, and be forced to do without, or try to borrow one from
someone else. I have even had people show up in one of my
seminars without so much as a pen or paper, presumably
expecting to spend all day learning something.

Drawing pictures to help you think logically is fairly
simple. It is more of an attitude and a habit than a skill. It has
nothing to do with artistic ability—it simply involves taking
information and putting it down in a concrete form for further
study and thought. As before, we will listen in (and, in this case,
look in) on the thoughts of a skilled thinker, to discover how he
or she uses graphic techniques to get control of problems and
solve them.

Here is a simple problem to think about. Try drawing some
kind of a diagram or sketch to help you understand and analyze
it. Think carefully about how you might arrange the available
information graphically, and what kind of a picture might contribute the most to your understanding.

EXAMPLE PROBLEM 5-1 (PICTURING)

Three playing cards lie face down on the table, arranged in a
row from left to right. We know the following things about
them.

1. The Jack is to the left of the Queen.
2. The Diamond is to the left of the Spade.
3. The King is to the right of the Heart.
4. The Spade is to the right of the King.

By representing these facts in picture form, determine the face
and suit of the card in each position—left, middle, and right. As
you work on it, be conscious of the process of thinking visually;

make it a familiar and comfortable process. Don't read further until you have given it a good try.

Ready to see and hear how the skilled thinker might approach this problem? Turn to the end of the chapter to see the sketch he or she drew. If you like, fill in the 'Xs' as you follow along.

Here is the internal monologue: "Well! A playing-card problem. Let me see . . . first, I need a reliable picture of what's going on. I'll just (!)draw three little rectangles in a row from left to right, to represent the left, middle, and right positions (picturing). Now, I have to start associating any facts I have with those positions. Let me see . . . it's kind of hard to decide where to begin because none of the facts tells me exactly where any one card goes. I can work by trial and error, but I might have to backtrack lots of times. I know—I'll make a checklist of all three faces and all three suits in a column to the left of my diagram, just below the sketch of the three cards (picturing). On the line running across from each face and each suit, I'll (!)put an 'X' below any position that I can rule out (fencing). By a process of elimination, I'll have a grid of 'Xs,' and the empty spaces should tell me which ones go where.

"Let me see, . . . the first fact—'the Jack is to the left of Queen'—tells me that the Jack can't be on the right, since it can't be on the left of anything else (stepping). So I'll put an 'X' under the right position, on the line across from the Jack. The Jack can only be on the left or in the center. Proceeding in the same way, fact number 2 tells me that the Spade can't be on the left. Number 3 tells me that the Heart can't be on the right. Number 4 tells me that the King can't be on the right. Now I see two 'Xs' under the right position for the faces. The King and the Jack are ruled out for the right position, so it must be the Queen. Now back to the list of facts. The first two facts aren't specific enough, because 'left' can mean either of two positions. But the third fact, 'the King is to the right of the

Heart' tells me that the King has to be in the center because the extreme right position is already occupied by the Queen. That also means that the Heart must be in the first position. Now we have the Queen on the right and the King in the center, so that puts the Jack of Hearts on the left. So the King of Diamonds must be in the center. Going from left to right, we have the Jack of Hearts, King of Diamonds, and the Queen must be a Spade. Let me go back and double-check this against the four facts I started with . . . yep—that's the solution.''

You might have found a shorter way to do it, either by trial and error, or by just filling in your diagram and drawing certain conclusions to fence it down quickly. Either way, I think you'll agree that a graphic version of the problem is enormously helpful in solving it. I hope you'll also agree that training yourself to pull out your pen at the slightest indication of the need for logical thinking would be a useful habit to form.

Let's try another problem.

EXAMPLE PROBLEM 5-2 (PICTURING)

We want to cook some vegetables for a period of 9 minutes, with no breaks. However, the only timepieces available are a 4-minute egg timer and a 7-minute egg timer. Neither timer has any markings on it, so they can only be used for starting and stopping. How is it possible to measure a continuous 9-minute period by combining these two timers? Try to work it out before reading further.

Ready to see and hear the expert thinker's approach? Here is a simple solution, with the diagram given at the end of the chapter. Advanced puzzle solvers will recognize that there is a more clever solution that the one given, but I've chosen this one because it makes it easier to illustrate the skill of picturing without introducing too many other techniques that might be confusing.

Here goes: "Let me see . . . two egg timers—a 4-minute one and a 7-minute one. How to time a 9-minute period? Think I'll (!)draw a sketch of this (picturing). I'll represent the 4-minute timer by a bar that's 4 units long. Next to that, I'll draw another bar that's 7 units long, to represent the 7-minute timer. Now I can draw, or visualize, various combinations of these bars, until I find a combination that adds up to 9 minutes. Let's see . . . if I run the 4-minute timer twice in a row, starting it together with the 7-minute timer, there's a 1-minute difference I can take advantage of. One minute before the second 4-minute period is over, the 7-minute timer runs out. Hmm . . . let me see . . . I know—I'll (!)start cooking the vegetables when the 7-minute timer runs out (stepping). That will be at the point where there is only 1 minute to go in the second round of the 4-minute timer. After that 1-minute period is up, I'll immediately turn over the 4-minute timer and start it again. When it runs out—after 5 minutes have elapsed—I'll turn it over once more for another 4 minutes. That will give me 1 minute plus 4 minutes plus 4 minutes, for a total of 9. All this thinking about food is making me hungry. Think I'll have lunch."

(Note to advanced puzzle fans: of course, the problem can be solved without having to wait 7 minutes for the 7-minute timer to finish. Just start the vegetables at the same time you start both timers; when the 7-minute timer is finished, there is 1 minute to go on the 4-minute timer. Just restart the 7-minute timer immediately and let it run until the 4-minute timer's 1-minute period is up. At that time, the 7-minute timer will have 1 minute's worth of sand at one end, and 8 minutes will have gone by. By reversing the 7-minute timer again and letting the 1 minute's worth of sand run out, you will have timed two 4-minute periods followed immediately by a 1-minute period.)

So there you have it. Two examples of how a diagram, sketch, or other graphic representation of a problem can help you think logically. Now try your hand at these practice problems. Use paper freely, and don't hesitate to backtrack or start fresh if you feel blocked. Try different kinds of diagrams until you find one that seems to support your thinking process effectively. You'll find solutions at the end of the chapter.

Practice Problem 5-1 (Picturing)

A bookworm decided to have lunch on a four-volume set of Mark Twain's works. The books were arranged on the shelf in volume order, going from left to right—*i.e.* Volume 1, Volume 2, Volume 3, and Volume 4. He started at the first page of Volume 1 and ate all the way through to the last page of Volume 4. The front and back covers of the books were each one-sixteenth of an inch thick, and the pages in each book took up exactly one inch. Question: how many inches did he cover in his eating binge? NOTE: be careful! Draw your diagram carefully, and reread the statement of the problem. Good luck!

Practice Problem 5-2 (Picturing)

This item appeared in a newspaper:

> The District Court today overturned the injunction forbidding police to enforce the mayor's directive to halt construction of X-rated theaters near churches.

Question: Would the leaders of the churches be happy about this, or not? Note: Try drawing a "ladder" diagram showing the precedence of each action in a hierarchy.

These simple problems have given you an opportunity to develop your skills at representing problems in visual form. If you don't already carry a pen with you wherever you go, make it a habit immediately. Train yourself to draw pictures whenever you confront a new problem, and use diagrams to explain your ideas to others. You'll soon find picturing to be such a worthwhile process that it will become a fundamental part of your logical problem-solving bag of tricks.

Solutions to Problems

Example Problem 5-1 (Picturing)

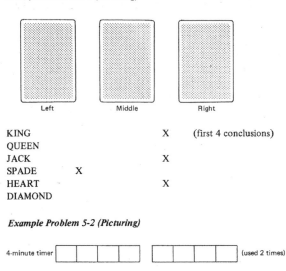

Left	Middle	Right

KING		X	(first 4 conclusions)
QUEEN			
JACK		X	
SPADE	X		
HEART		X	
DIAMOND			

Example Problem 5-2 (Picturing)

4-minute timer ☐☐☐☐ ☐☐☐☐ (used 2 times)

7-minute timer ☐☐☐☐☐☐☐ 1-minute interval

Practice Problem 5-1 (Picturing)

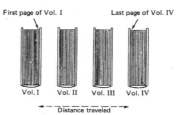

First page of Vol. I   Last page of Vol. IV

Vol. I   Vol. II   Vol. III   Vol. IV

Distance traveled

     He ate through 6 covers (one-sixteenth inch each), and 2 stacks of pages (1 inch each), for a total of 2 and three-eighths inches.

Practice Problem 5-2 (Picturing):

ACTION	EVALUATION
District Court Overturns Injunction	positive
Injunction To Prevent Police From Enforcing	negative
Police Enforce Directive To Halt Construction	positive
X-Rated Theaters Nearby	negative
Churches	positive

The action would be positive for the churches.

38

REPHRASING

Often a problem or situation seems overly complex or hard to understand, simply because the words someone else uses to describe it to you are complicated, vague, or confusing. By *rephrasing* the problem in your own words, you can get it organized in your mind. You can simplify it and get a firmer grasp of it.

Here is an example of a simple problem.

EXAMPLE PROBLEM 6-1 (REPHRASING)

How much is two-thirds of one-half?

If you recall your junior-high school math, you remember that this problem calls for a routine procedure dealing with the manipulation of fractions.

You say something like: "Two-thirds of one-half . . . that means I have to multiply two fractions together. Let me see—what's that procedure? Multiply the top number of one fraction by the top number of the other and use the product as the top number of the new fraction. Then, multiply the bottom number of one by the bottom number of the other and use that product as the bottom number of the new fraction. So, two times one equals two—the top number of the answer; and three times two equals six—the bottom number of the answer. I come up with two over six, or two sixths. Now I see that two sixths can be reduced to one third. So the answer is: two-thirds of one-half is one-third."

Fairly simple yes? Now consider this problem: How much is half of two-thirds? The answer fairly jumps out at you: Half of two-thirds is one-third, of course. This is exactly the same problem you just solved, simply worded in reverse order. Just by changing the way we stated the problem, by *rephrasing* it, we have made it simpler, easier to understand, and easier to solve. Rephrasing is one of the most powerful thinking strategies available to you, and it is fairly easy to start using it more frequently.

Resolve right now that you will never again accept another person's phrasing of a problem situation unless you have thought about various other ways to phrase it, and determine that the other person's way can help you to think about it clearly. Make it an automatic habit to restate, to paraphrase, to clarify a problem statement until you feel comfortable with your understanding of the problem.

Let's try another example of rephrasing, this time with a simple problem that invites *creative thinking* as well as sequential thinking.

EXAMPLE PROBLEM 6-2 (REPHRASING)

A man playing golf drove his first ball so well that it rolled right onto the green. From a distance, something about the ball looked peculiar. When he arrived at the pin, he noticed that the ball had rolled right into an empty paper bag that had apparently blown onto the green. With the ball inside the bag, he couldn't figure out how to sink the putt for his birdie. Then he suddenly realized how to do it. What was his solution? Think about it before you read further.

How did you make out? In any case, let's tune in on the thoughts of our friend the logical thinker, to see how he or she would attack it.

"Hmm . . . I don't want to waste a shot getting the ball out of the bag so I can knock it into the hole. What shall I do? Let me see—I want to get the ball into the hole. First, though, I want to get it out of the bag. (!)Or maybe I just want to get rid of the bag (rephrasing) . . . I've got it! I'll light a match, set fire to the paper bag, and let it burn to ashes. Then I'll just blow away the ashes and sink the putt without any hindrance."

In this imaginary dilemma, we can see that rephrasing the problem helped to find a workable solution. It enabled the thinker to make the creative leap from trying to hit the ball to getting rid of the bag. This is a good illustration of the intimate connections that can and should exist between "logical" thinking and "creative" thinking.

Make it a habit to talk your thoughts out loud in a problem-solving situation whenever possible. If you're alone, or with compatible people, just start verbalizing different thoughts or fragments of thoughts. This kind of *loud* thinking gets your mind working in a sequential mode, and helps you start moving toward a solution, however erratic or uncertain that motion might be. It is very important in logical problem solving to get moving and to escape from a dead-center position in which you simply sit and stare at the problem.

Let's try another example of rephrasing, this time with a problem stated in a very intricate, slippery way.

EXAMPLE PROBLEM 6-3 (REPHRASING)

A man is standing before a portrait hanging on the wall. He points to the portrait and makes the following statement about the person represented in the portrait: "Brothers and sisters have I none, but this man's father is my father's son." Your problem is to find out who the person in the portrait is, *i.e.* how is he related to the speaker? Take a pen and paper and analyze the situation, making a special effort to rephrase the problem or parts of the problem so you can deal with it more clearly. Don't read any further until you feel you have an answer, or until you're ready to see how a skilled logical thinker would attack it.

Okay? Now, let's listen in on the thoughts of a person skilled in logical thinking. Again the editorial symbol (!)is a signal that points out something the thinker is about to do that will help him or her understand the problem more clearly.

"Hmm, let me see . . . the thing is worded in a kind of *circular* way—it doesn't hold still. It seems to turn back on itself, without offering a clear-cut place to start. I'll see if I can (!)change a few of the key terms to make it more understandable (rephrasing). 'Brothers and sisters have I none' tells me that the speaker is an only child. If he is an only child, then the phrase 'my father's son' can only refer to the speaker himself (stepping). I can (!)substitute these simpler terms for the confusing statements given in the problem. I can express it in the following way: 'I am an only child. This man's father is me.' So, the person represented in the portrait is the speaker's son."

How did your answer compare to the one given here? How successful were you at rephrasing the problem? Please don't be discouraged if you found this problem difficult, or if you didn't come up with the correct solution. This particular problem is rather tricky, and anyway, the learning process must proceed in small stages. Just be sure that you understand the solution as given, and that you understand how the logical thinker came upon it.

In particular, notice that the logical thinker did not simply jump at the answer in a single leap. As we followed the internal reasoning process, we could see a definite *sequence* of steps. First, the thinker clarified the role of the person speaking—he was an only child. This fact, clearly understood, paved the way to the *if-then reasoning process* that concluded that the speaker was talking about his own son.

This step-wise nature of logical thinking is the single most important point you need to understand. People who are skilled at what is commonly called *intuitive thinking*, but have trouble with logical thinking, all suffer from the same handicap: lack of patience with small steps. The intuitive thinker likes to move in large, exciting jumps—flashes of insight, inspirations, global concepts, overall impressions, notions that feel right. He or she has very little patience with the disciplined, linear, step-by-step procedure of organizing the elements of a situation and moving from one known fact to another. While the free-wheeling intuitive process is ideal for certain kinds of problems, it fails dismally in the face of problems that demand a logical, systematic approach. The intuitive thinker must learn to respect the disciplined, linear approach and to capitalize on its advantages in those situations where it works best.

Now, it's time for you to try your hand at a few practice problems that invite you to use the technique of rephrasing. As you approach the following problems, keep in mind that a clear statement of what you are trying to do is half the battle. What is the outcome you want? What are you trying to find out? Try to simplify, reduce, restate, paraphrase, or explain the problem from various angles until you find one that will help you really understand it. While you're about it, don't limit yourself to just the technique of rephrasing. Use your pen and paper to draw pictures or make diagrams that help you to organize the problem. Talk out loud to yourself or to another person if

possible. Above all, proceed with patience. Don't try to solve
the problem with one heroic leap. Be content to break it down
into small pieces, and operate on one piece at a time. As you
become more confident, you will become more skillful, more
logical, and more organized. You'll find solutions at the end of
the chapter.

Practice Problem 6-1 (Rephrasing)

A mouse was nibbling on a long, straight piece of cheese. One-
third of an hour after he started, his friend joined him, nibbling
at the other end. It took another one-third of an hour for the
two of them to finish eating the cheese, both nibbling at
the same speed. If they had started nibbling together, and the
second one quit at the point when only the middle one-third
remained, how long would it take the first one to eat the rest
of the cheese, and how long in all would it take them to finish
it?

Practice Problem 6-2 (Rephrasing)

Three children were suspected of stealing an apple pie from the
kitchen. When asked which one did it, they answered as follows.

1. A said, "I didn't take it."
2. B said, "A is lying."
3. C said, "B is lying."

If only one of their statements is true, which child took the pie?
Hint: Try testing all three assumptions in turn, *i.e.* that A did it,
then that B did it, and then that C did it.

Solutions to Problems

Practice Problem 6-1 (Rephrasing):
The second situation is, for all practical purposes, the same as the first. One mouse can eat one-third of the cheese in one-third of an hour. When they worked together, they ate two-thirds of it in one-third of an hour. In the second situation, it would take the two of them one-third of an hour to eat two-thirds of the cheese, and it would take the first one one-third of an hour to finish the remaining one-third of it. In either case, it takes them two-thirds of an hour to eat the cheese.

Practice Problem 6-2 (Rephrasing):
If only one of the statements is true, then any assumption about which boy took the pie that results in more than one true statement must be invalid. Let's test the possibilities. If A took the pie, then statement number 1 is false; that makes statement number 2 true; and statement number 3 must be false. This arrangement is logically consistent. A might be guilty; let's check on the other boys.

If B took the pie, then statement number 1 is true, statement number 2 is false, and statement number 3 is true. There can only be one true statement, so B did not take the pie.

If C took the pie, then statement number 1 is true, statement number 2 is false, and statement number 3 is true. This is also invalid.

Therefore, boy A took the pie.

7

FENCING

One reason why you may sometimes feel overwhelmed by a problem is that it may appear to be bigger, more complex, and more confusing than it really is. The technique of *fencing* the problem down to a smaller size can help you regain a feeling of confidence and mastery. It is sometimes said that "inside a big problem, there is usually a small problem struggling to get out. ' By looking at the problem carefully, and not getting distracted by the way someone first presents it to you, you may be able to put your finger on the one key factor that lies at the heart. Deal with that key factor, and you often can solve the problem effectively, without ever having to get tangled up in all the other side issues. Fencing is a *reductive* strategy; it seeks to condense the problem to its very essence so you can resolve it most efficiently.

Let's look at some examples of the technique of fencing. Here is a good problem.

EXAMPLE PROBLEM 7-1 (FENCING)

Picture a 3 X 3-grid square, *i.e.* three squares by three squares. How can you arrange the nine digits from 1 to 9, assigning one number to each of the nine squares in such a way that each row, each column, and both diagonals total up to exactly 15? Before reading further, take your pen and paper and experiment with the problem. Try to discover a way to fence the problem—to reduce it down to manageable proportions. Test various possibilities to see if you can reduce a rule that governs the arrangement.

(Put the numbers 1, 2, 3, 4, 5, 6, 7, 8, and 9 in the proper boxes.)

Ready to look at the logical thinker's solution? Refer to the diagram at the end of the chapter.

Let me see . . . how can I (!)restate this? I have to put the nine numbers in groups of three, and each group has to add up to 15 (rephrasing). There are three rows, three columns, and two diagonals. Each number gets included in more than one group of three, so I have to make sure the groups are all compatible with one another . . . . Hmm, how can I (!)narrow it down, so I don't have to try all those combinations to find the right one? Well, for one thing, let me look at that center position—the middle box in the matrix. There must be something special about that number because it gets added to every other number in the grid. Let's try some possibilities—suppose I put a 1 in the center. Would that work? Well, (!)if I add it to 2 in some other box I only get 3, and there isn't any other number large enough to bring the total to 15. (!)So 1 is out and (!)2 is out for the same reason (stepping). Let's see, what about high numbers. If I put a 9 in the center spot and I put 8 in any other box, I've already overshot the total of 15 before I even add in the third number. So I know that 1 won't work, 9 won't work,

2 won't work, 8 won't work . . . . I wonder if there is only one acceptable number for the center? Yes, the only possible choice for the center square is 5. The number 4 and any smaller number are too low, and 6 and any higher numbers are too high. So I've narrowed down the possible choices to one number, 5 (fencing). Now let me start filling in the other squares on a trial basis and see what happens . . . "

The rest of the problem yields fairly easily to a straightforward process of checking the positions of various numbers and making sure the totals are correct in all directions. Once you have done that, you can come up with an arrangement of numbers that satisfies the basic condition of providing totals of 15.

From this simple process, you can see how powerful a technique fencing can be. Just think of the number of trial-and-error attempts you would have to make to check out most of the combinations of numbers involved, hoping to find a combination that works. Using the process of fencing, you can reduce the number of combinations you have to try to a very small number. This gives you a feeling of mastery over the problem, and it increases your confidence in your ability to think clearly and logically.

How about another example? Here's one that seems highly mathematical at first, and yet it can be fenced quite easily by thinking carefully about the relationships involved. Take a pen and paper, and give it a try before reading further.

EXAMPLE PROBLEM 7-2 (FENCING)

A flock of seagulls came in to land on a row of wooden pilings. We don't know how many seagulls there were, and we don't know how many pilings there were, but we can find out from the following information. When the birds tried to land so that each piling only had one bird perched on it, there was one bird left over, with no place to land. But when they tried to land with two birds per piling, there was one unoccupied piling. How many birds and how many pilings were involved in this episode?

Ready? Again, let's listen to the thoughts of a disciplined mind at work.

"Well, let me see . . . birds and pilings . . . Is this a mathematical problem, or can I solve it by cutting it down to size? First, let me try (!)fencing it in as much as possible. Let me see . . . the way it's worded tells me there is one more bird than pilings. But if I double-up the birds, I have one less pair of birds than I have pilings (rephrasing). Hmm . . . something tells me I'm dealing with a fairly small number of items here . . . why do I think that? If I cut the number of birds in half, and that number is still only one less than the number of pilings . . . yes, it has to be a fairly small number of birds and pilings, maybe less than ten (fencing). Maybe I should (!)try all the combinations of birds and pilings, starting with one and working up (itemizing). Let me see if that works . . . one piling and two birds doesn't work—none left over. Oh, the number of birds has to be even (fencing), so I can (!)skip over two pilings and three birds and try the next combination. Let me see . . . three pilings and four birds—that works! If four birds try to land on three pilings, there's one extra bird; and if they double up, the two pairs of birds leave one piling unoccupied. So 3 and 4 is a solution. But (!)are there other combinations that might work? Let me see . . . five pilings and six birds? No, there would be two pilings left over. I can see that as the number of birds and pilings gets larger and larger, there are more and more pilings left over, so it can't work for large numbers. The only solution is three birds and four pilings."

I hope you were able to anticipate this solution, and that you were able to use the technique of fencing effectively. If not, however, you need not get discouraged. Just by seeing how it is done by a skilled thinker, you are learning something. If you've had difficulty with logical processes in the past, it's reasonable to expect fairly slow progress at first. Little by little, you will develop a feel for the process of organizing and controlling information in your mind, and the more examples you read, the more you will be able to apply the techniques used in the examples.

Now, try your hand. The following puzzle is one you can solve with the aid of the technique of fencing. Before you attack it, here is a helpful hint: At first glance, it looks like a mathematical puzzle, but it really isn't. You don t have to do any involved calculations—just look for a *strategy* that will quickly eliminate the uncertainty involved. If you don't get it soon, come back and reread this hint.

Practice Problem 7-1 (Fencing)

You have 10 bags of gold coins. The bags are numbered from 1 to 10. Each bag contains 10 coins, and each coin is supposed to weigh 1 ounce. However, you suspect that one of the bags is light, *i.e.* each of the coins it contains weighs only nine-tenths of an ounce instead of 1 ounce. You have an accurate weighing scale available, but you will only be allowed to make one weighing with it. How can you figure out which bag has the light coins by making only one weighing with the scale?

Practice Problem 7-2 (Fencing)

Four playing cards are stacked up on the table, face down. They are an Ace, a King, a Queen, and a Jack. They represent all four suits. By progressively eliminating possibilities, can you fence the problem down so you can determine which face and suit are in each position? Here are the key facts:

1. The King is not the top card, but it is closer to the top than either the Ace or the Jack.
2. The Heart is above the Club.
3. The King is not a Heart, and it is not a Club.
4. The Ace is neither a Spade nor a Diamond.
5. The Diamond is below the Club.

How did you make out? I hope that by proceeding in careful steps and progressively fencing in the problem, you have developed a greater sense of confidence in your logical processes. As you face various other problems from day to day, make a point to look for opportunities to fence them down to manageable proportions. Don't give up on my problem unless you have made an effort to reduce it. Fencing doesn't always guarantee you a simple solution because many problems are not simple. But it often will help you get the problem under control and give you a greater sense of confidence and mastery.

Solutions to Problems

Example Problem 7-1 (Fencing)

2	9	4
7	5	3
6	1	8

Practice Problem 7-1 (Fencing)
Take 1 coin from bag 1, 2 coins from bag 2, 3 coins from bag 3, and so on up to 10 coins from bag 10. Keeping them in separate stacks, put them on the scale and weigh them. If they weigh exactly 1 ounce each, the total will be 1+2+3+4+5+6+7+8+9+10 ounces, or 55 ounces. If one bag is light, the total will be less

than 55 ounces, by an amount—measured in tenths of an ounce—equal to the number of the bag that is light. That is, if the sampled coins weigh four-tenths of an ounce less than 55 ounces, you know that bag 4 is light because you took 4 coins from that bag.

Practice Problem 7-2 (Fencing)
From the top of the stack down, the cards are as follows.

> Queen of Hearts
> King of Spades
> Ace of Clubs
> Jack of Diamonds

ITEMIZING

One of the easiest and most effective ways to get control of a confused situation is simply to *itemize* the variables involved. You may be surprised to see how many times the simple process of taking a pen and making a list of the key factors involved can bring the problem clearly into focus. Despite the cynical comments many people make about making lists, it remains one of the most useful of all logical thought processes. For example, working from a list of things to do every day gives you the power to decide how you can best spend your time, and which of the many demands on your time represent the best possible payoffs.

Similarly, when you are discussing some projects with another person, it helps enormously to itemize the various things to be done. You can also itemize the various problem areas you might encounter, the various issues to be resolved in carrying out the project, and the various people whose support you must enlist. If you don't already use this process of itemizing the factors involved in situations, begin now to make it a reliable and permanent habit. In this chapter, we will solve a few puzzle problems with the aid of the tactic of itemizing so you can see how well it works and how straightforward a skill it can become.

EXAMPLE PROBLEM 8-1 (ITEMIZING)

If you flip two coins at the same time, what are the chances that they will both come up heads? Or, in other words, if you flip them many times, what percentage of the times will you get two heads?

Try to discover how you can use the technique of itemizing to understand the problem thoroughly. Think about this with the aid of your pen and paper before reading the expert thinker's approach.

Ready to tune in on our friend the logical thinker? Refer to the figure at the end of the chapter.

"Let me see, flipping a coin. Two at a time . . . each coin can come up one of two ways, and there are only so many combinations of heads and tails. First, I have to (!)figure out how many possible combinations of heads and tails I can get with the two coins (stepping, itemizing). Then I just have to (!)count the number of those combinations that consist of two heads (itemizing). When I have those two numbers, I just divide the number of "head-head" pairs by the total number of pairs that can turn up and I'll have the percentage of times two heads can be expected to come up. That's the same as the "probability" of two heads.

"Well, let me (!)itemize the possible combinations . . . with two coins, I can get 'heads-heads,' 'heads-tails,' 'tails-heads,' and 'tails-tails' (itemizing). By this I see that two heads can come up once out of the four possibilities, so if all the combinations are equally likely to come up, two heads will come up 25 percent of the time. In other words, the probability of flipping two heads is .25, or 25 percent. Wonder if that's right? Maybe I'll test it by flipping two coins a hundred times or so . . . no—think I'll go to lunch instead."

How did you make out with this problem? This is a very interesting one, and if you didn't solve it at first you needn't be discouraged. This kind of thought process, especially dealing with probabilities, is unfamiliar to many people. Nevertheless, it is a useful process. You may have hit a blank wall at first, not knowing exactly how to get into the problem. Itemizing the possibilities may seem to be a rather novel way to attack it; it isn't the kind of problem that comes along and says "Please itemize me." You have to think carefully about each of the seven logical tactics to see which ones might help you with a given problem.

Let's try another problem. Again, take your pen and paper and apply the itemizing process to help you solve it. Work on it carefully before reading further.

EXAMPLE PROBLEM 8-2 (ITEMIZING)

A lady went into the post office, gave the clerk a dollar, and said "I want exactly a dollar's worth of stamps. Make it some two-cent stamps, 10 times as many one-cent stamps as two-cent stamps, and the rest in five-cent stamps. How many of each kind of stamp did she buy?

Now, let's see how the logical thinker tackled this problem. Refer to the diagram at the end of the chapter.

"Hmm . . . exactly a dollar? No change left? Well . . . that means there must be some exact relationship between the numbers of stamps and their denominations that multiplies out to exactly 100 cents (rephrasing). We just have to check out various combinations to see which ones work (stepping, itemizing). Let me see . . . she buys two-cent stamps, one-cent stamps, and five-cent stamps, so we have three categories to work with. Let me (!)write those down in a column (itemizing). Then, I'll make two other columns—one for the number of stamps of each kind, and one for the cost of those particular stamps. Let me see, how many 2-cent stamps can she buy—

seems like quite a few . . . no! For every 2-cent stamp, she buys ten 1-cent stamps. So she's committed to buying two's and one's in 'lots' that cost 12 cents. Hmm, it's shaping up now. She buys a certain number of lots of two's and one's at 12 cents per lot. That quantity, multiplied by 12 cents, takes up part of the dollar, and the rest has to be taken up exactly by a certain multiple of 5 cents.

"So, I think it boils down to (!)finding a multiple of 12 and a multiple of 5 that give us a total of 100 cents (fencing). Now, the 5-cent stamp imposes certain limits on things—there can only be 5 cents worth, 10 cents worth, and so on. Aha! We have to find a multiple of 12 cents that ends in a five or a zero, in order for the 5-cent stamps to give us a total of 100 cents. The only multiple of 12 that will work is 5—that is, 5 lots of stamps at 12 cents per lot gives 60 cents. Then we can use the other 40 cents to buy eight 5-cent stamps. Let me (!)double-check —five 2-cent stamps, plus fifty 1-cent stamps, and eight 5-cent stamps, for a total of one dollar. Got it!"

Okay, now it's your turn. Here are some easy problems you can use to practice your skill at itemizing. You'll find the solutions at the end of the chapter.

Practice Problem 8-1 (Itemizing)

Look at the following figure. It contains 16 squares, doesn't it? But does it? Look closely and you'll see that it has 17 squares, including the big square that forms the boundary. But wait! There are other squares contained in the figure besides those that measure one-by-one. There are also two-by-two squares, . . . well, how many squares are there in the figure?

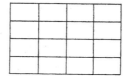

Practice Problem 8-2 (Itemizing)

What is the minimum number of coins I must have in my pocket to be able to go into a shop and make a purchase, paying the exact amount for any price ranging from one cent to a dollar, and which coins do I need?

I hope you're finding the technique of itemizing convenient, natural, and useful. Train yourself to spot those situations in which putting things down in orderly fashion can help you or others to think more effectively. Of course, be sure to combine the tactic of itemizing with all the others you've learned to get maximum benefits from all of them.

Solutions to Problems

Example Problem 8-1 (Itemizing)
Draw a diagram something like this.

Coin 1	Coin 2
Heads	Heads
Heads	Tails
Tails	Heads
Tails	Tails

Number of possible combinations:	4
Number of times two heads comes up:	1
Probability of two heads:	1 in 4, or 25%

Example Problem 8-2 (Itemizing)
Draw a diagram something like this.

Kind of Stamp	Number	Cost
two-cent	x	x times two cents
one-cent	10 times x	x times ten times, one cent
five-cent	?	100 cents minus 2x minus 10x

Then, try different guesses for x until you find a combination that works exactly.

Practice Problem 8-1 (Itemizing):

1. 1 x 1 squares: 16
2. 2 x 2 squares: 9
3. 3 x 3 squares: 4
4. 4 x 4 squares: <u>1</u>
        Total: <u>30</u>

Practice Problem 8-2 (Itemizing)

Make a diagram something like this.

Price	Coin Required
1-4 cents	1-4 pennies
5 cents	1 nickel
6-9 cents	1 nickel, 1-4 pennies
10 cents	1 dime
11-14 cents	1 dime, 1-4 pennies
15 cents	1 dime, 1 nickel
16-19 cents	1 dime, 1 nickel, 1-4 pennies
20 cents	2 dimes
21-24 cents	2 dimes, 1-4 pennies
25 cents	1 quarter
26-29 cents	1 quarter, 1-4 pennies
30 cents	1 quarter, 1 nickel
31-34 cents	1 quarter, 1 nickel, 1-4 pennies
35 cents	1 quarter, 1 dime
- etc. -	
50 cents	1 half-dollar
- etc. -	
90 cents	1 half-dollar, 1 quarter, 1 dime, 1 nickel
99 cents	1 half-dollar, 1 quarter, 1 dime, 1 nickel, 4 pennies
1 dollar	1 half-dollar, 1 quarter, 2 dimes, 1 nickel

Total number of coins: 9—4 pennies, 1 nickel, 2 dimes, 1 quarter, 1 half-dollar.

Note that if you used 1 dime and 2 nickels instead of 2 dimes to make 20 cents, you would need an extra penny to reach 1 dollar. With 2 dimes and 1 nickel, you can actually exceed 1 dollar—$1.04.

CHAINING

A rather sophisticated logical technique—but not a difficult one—is *chaining*, or laying out various options in the form of a diagram that shows how some options precede others. Chaining is useful in those situations where you are faced with a number of choices, and you need to make sure you have accounted for all of them. You may also need to get the choices arranged in some meaningful way so you can understand them and discuss them with someone else.

One of the useful diagrams for chaining is the *tree diagram.* This is simply a sketch that shows a group of branching lines, one for each major option you want to consider. Some options will have *suboptions* associated with them. These you represent with other lines that branch off further from the main lines. To illustrate the use of a *logic tree*, let's suppose you wake up on a Sunday morning and want to decide how to spend a leisurely, enjoyable day. You think about such considerations as whether to spend it alone or with a friend, whether to take a short trip somewhere or stay around home, and how long a day to make it. These options might look like this, when expressed in words.

1. How much time?
   a. Half day
   b. Full day, but not evening
   c. Full day, including evening

2. Company?
   a. Just me
   b. Call a friend
3. Distance?
   a. Stay around home
   b. Take a drive

Here you have three major options and each option has two or more suboptions. Suboptions can also have suboptions, such as which friend to invite, what to do around home—play games, watch a movie, got to the park, etc., and where to go on a trip—mountains, beach, a favorite resort, a charming little town, etc. Note that some suboptions only apply to certain major options. For example, you cannot stay around home and also visit a charming little town fifty miles away. So you must make your decision in *stages*. You have to narrow down the options progressively, moving in a logical pattern.

Now, let's see how your chaining process might look when expressed in the form of a decision tree.

Note that a multilevel decision problem like this fans out to many individual choices. In this case, you get three primary options, multiplied by two suboptions, and each of the suboptions is multiplied by whatever number of activities you want to consider. You could easily have 20 or 30 different choices. Chaining them together can help you to account for all of them and think about them in a systematic way.

Now, here is an example of a problem that invites the use of the logical tactic of chaining. Take your pen and paper and give it a try. Draw a logic tree that shows the choices the two players have as they take turns. Then read the expert thinker's attack, referring to the diagram at the end of the chapter.

EXAMPLE PROBLEM 9-1 (CHAINING)

A curious little two-person game involves the use of five coins, arranged on the table to form a circle, like this.

The two players take turns picking up coins and the person who manages to pick up the last coin wins the game. The rules are simple: You can pick up either one coin or two coins when it's your move, *but* you can only take two coins if they are touching each other. You cannot pick up two coins that are separated; you can only take one of them. Question: To have the best chance of winning, should you be the first person to move or the second?

Ready? Here's how our friend the logical thinker attacked it.

"Hmm . . . a game using coins, the object is to pick up the last coin—whatever it takes to do that. Seems like the person who moves first has the best chance of winning because he or she would probably have more options. But, maybe that isn't true. Let me (!)account for all the moves and submoves by drawing a logic tree (picturing, chaining). It should be a fairly simple diagram, because with five coins the game will be over in just a few moves. Well, let me see what it looks like. I'll start with the first player, and diagram his or her possible moves—oh, it's really simple; the first player can pick up one or two coins, that's all there is to it. So, I'll (!)have two main branches to my diagram, showing the first player's two possibilities (picturing). Now, from each of those two branches, I'll show the second player's two possible moves, and from each of *those* branches, I'll show what the first player can do when it's his turn again.

"So, here's my diagram. [See solution at the end of the chapter.] Now, let's start to evaluate the best moves (stepping). I'll also (!)take these five coins and put them on the table so I'll have a physical model of the game to work from (picturing). Let me see, if the first player takes one coin, what can the second player do? Aha! If the second player takes the two middle coins from the remaining ring of coins, that leaves player number one with a 'split.' (!)He can only pick up one of the two separated coins, leaving the other for the second player, who will win (stepping). Hmm, what do you know about that? Well, the first player has another option—he can pick up two coins on the first move. What happens then? Hmm . . . if he picks up two coins, that leaves a group of three for the second player. Oh, yes . . . the second player then picks up the middle coin from the group of three, again leaving the first player with a split. That's remarkable! So, the second player can win every time if he makes the correct moves, no matter what the first player does. That's certainly counterintuitive, but it makes sense when you look at the logic of it. So, I'd rather be the second player to move."

See how the simple tactic of chaining can change the way you look at something? Drawing a logic tree often creates a sense of order in an ambiguous situation, thus giving you an insight into the problem you might otherwise not have had.

Your diagram and the chaining process you use don't neces-
sarily have to be formal or elaborate. By combining the tactic of
chaining with other tactics such as picturing, fencing, and stepping, you can often cut the problem down to manageable size
so it isn't even necessary to explore all of the options and suboptions. Here are some practice problems you can try where a
simplifying approach can make the chaining technique go a long
way.

Practice Problem 9-1 (Chaining)

A man wants to cross a river and he must take three items with
him. The items are a wolf, a goat, and a giant cabbage. He has a
boat, but the boat is only large enough to hold him and one of
the items so he must transport them across the river one at a
time. He is further handicapped by the fact that he cannot leave
the wolf and the goat together unattended, since the wolf will
eat the goat. Nor can he leave the goat and the cabbage together
unattended, since the goat will eat the cabbage. It is permissible,
however, for him to leave the wolf and the cabbage together
because the wolf is not interested in the cabbage. Question: By
what sequence of crossings does he succeed in getting himself,
the boat, the wolf, the goat, and the cabbage, safely to the
opposite side of the river?

Practice Problem 9-2 (Chaining)

You have an 8-gallon container full of water. You also have an
empty 3-gallon container and an empty 5-gallon container.
None of the containers has any measuring scales; in fact you
have no way of measuring the water at all, except by filling
either of the two empty containers completely full. Nevertheless, it is possible, merely by pouring the water back and forth

between containers, to add and subtract quantities of water until you have divided the 8-gallon quantity into two 4-gallon quantities. How can you do this?

By now, I hope you're feeling fairly comfortable with the tactic of chaining, and in fact with all of the linear, sequential processes we have been studying. The more often you see them used, and the more often you put them to use in your own thinking processes, the greater your skill will become.

Solutions to Problems

Example Problem 9-1 (Chaining)

Practice Problem 9-1 (Chaining)

1. First, the man takes the goat across the river, leaving the wolf and cabbage behind. (Alternatively, he could have taken the cabbage, with the same eventual solution.)
2. He leaves the goat on the far side and returns in the empty boat.
3. Then he takes the wolf over to the far side, exchanges the wolf for the goat, and brings the goat back to the near side.
4. He leaves the goat on the near side and takes the cabbage across.
5. He leaves the wolf and the cabbage on the far side and returns in the empty boat.
6. He then takes the goat over to the far side and he is finished.

Practice Problem 9-2 (Chaining)
Make a chart like the following, and proceed to fill in the status
of each container after each pouring step.

Step	3-Gallon Has	5-Gallon Has	8-Gallon Has
1	0	0	8 (start)
2	0	5	3 (fill 5)
3	3	2	3 (fill 3 from 5)
4	0	2	6 (empty 3 into 8)
5	2	0	6 (empty 5 into 3)
6	2	5	1 (fill 5 again)
7	3	4	1 ("top off" 3)
8	0	4	4 (empty 3 into 8)

JUMPING THE TRACK

The problem-solving tactic of *jumping the track* is one of the most useful of our seven key tactics, and yet it is the most difficult to explain. It is easy to demonstrate how to do it in a specific instance, and yet it is virtually impossible to prescribe a formula, or a recipe for it. In fact, it is not really a *logical* tactic as such, but rather a tactic that enhances the use of the other logical tactics. To jump the track, as a problem-solving technique, means to abandon your current approach and try something altogether different. It means, figuratively, to stop trying to dig the hole deeper, and to start digging in a new place altogether. It also means staying alert when you size up a problem and not letting yourself be drawn into the obvious path without considering various possibilities.

Because jumping the track is virtually impossible to define, let's just study a few examples to get the feel of the process. Let's listen in as our friend the logical thinker attacks a problem that calls for abandoning a fixed line of attack and jumping to another approach. Using your pen and paper, give the next problem a try before you read the solution.

EXAMPLE PROBLEM 10-1 (JUMPING THE TRACK)

Six ordinary drinking glasses are in a row on the table. The first three are filled with water and the last three are empty. By handling and moving only one glass, it is possible to change this arrangement so that no full glass is next to another full glass, and no empty glass is next to another empty glass. How is this done?

Let's hear from the logical thinker. Refer to the diagram at the end of the chapter.

"Hmm . . . you can only move one glass? That seems like a very severe limitation. Well, let me first (!)make a diagram (picturing). If I understand correctly, the situation looks something like this: [See diagram at end of chapter.] "Let me see . . . (!)if I could produce a situation where the glasses were 'full, empty, full, empty, full, empty,' I'd have it (rephrasing). But how can I do that if I only move . . . wait! The word *move* is the key. (!)I don't have to relocate it, all I have to do is relocate its *contents* (jumping the track). If I can move the water from the middle full glass to the middle empty glass, I'll have it. It's easy—just pick up the middle full one, pour its water into the middle empty one, and put it back in its original position. Ha! I'm so clever, I amaze myself sometimes."

Did you notice the sudden turn of the thinker's attack? He or she shifted attention from the glasses to the water. The problem then, was no longer "how to move the glasses," but "how to move the water." I know of no way to put that process into a formula or a procedure. What goes on in your brain when you jump the track is an absolute mystery to psychologists. They know it happens, and call it an *insight leap*, but they have no idea how your brain does it. This is one of the great mysteries of the human mind, and it is one of the most precious faculties you and I possess. It is the basis of great scientific breakthroughs and an important part of creative thinking.

Let's take a look at one more example, and then you can have fun trying your hand—or, more correctly, your mind—at a few of them.

EXAMPLE PROBLEM 10-2 (JUMPING THE TRACK)

How many months of the year have 31 days? How many have 30 days? Finally, how many months have 28 days?

Let's hear from our friend the expert thinker.

"Hmm . . . how does the old rhyme go? 'Thirty days hath September, April, June and November. All the rest have thirty-one, except February, which has twenty-eight, except when leap year gives it twenty-nine.' That means four months are thirty days long. Allowing one more for February, that leaves seven months with thirty-one days. Only February has twenty-eight days . . . hmm . . . (!)wa-a-a-i-t a minute . . . o-o-o-h-h! I get it—it's a trick! (insight leap) All twelve months have twenty-eight days. Most of them have more, but they all have twenty-eight. Very sneaky, but they didn't put one over on me!"

Again, a leap of insight that utterly defies analysis or description. It would seem, at first thought, that if we can't analyze and describe this leap of insight, we can't very well teach it to others, or that we can't very well practice it and improve on it. This is not entirely true. If you observe this leap-of-insight phenomenon often enough on the part of creative, effective thinkers, you can begin to develop an intuitive sense of what it is and how it works. By exposing yourself to problem-solving situations that invite you to jump the track, you can increase your alertness to new possibilities. Here are a couple of problems for practice. Keep your wits about you, and stay alert for the unusual.

Practice Problem 10-1 (Jumping the Track)

I needed a small supply of a certain item for my weekend home improvement project. I went to the hardware store to see what kinds they had and how much they cost. The clerk said, "One will cost you 50 cents, 50 will cost you a dollar, and 100 will cost you a dollar and fifty cents." What would I have been buying that would have such a strange quantity-pricing pattern?"

Practice Problem 10-2 (Jumping the Track)

A bottle and a cork together cost $1.10. The bottle cost $1.00 more than the cork cost. How much did the cork cost? The answer is *not* 10 cents. Think it over carefully.

Practice Problem 10-3 (Jumping the Track)

Why does the barber in Oatmeal, Nebraska say, "I would rather shave ten skinny men than one fat man?"

Solutions to Problems

Example Problem 10-1 (Jumping the Track)

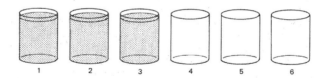

1   2   3   4   5   6

Practice Problem 10-1 (Jumping the Track)
I was buying house numbers. They cost fifty cents per digit.

Practice Problem 10-2 (Jumping the Track)
Don't fall into the trap of simply subtracting ten cents from $1.10. That would give $1.00 for the bottle and 10 cents for the cork, which is a difference of 90 cents, not one dollar. The correct answer is 5 cents for the cork and $1.05 for the bottle.

Practice Problem 10-3 (Jumping the Track)
The barber would make ten times as much money shaving ten men as he would shaving one man, fat or skinny.

11

PUTTING IT TOGETHER

Well, I hope you've found our little excursion through logical thinking enjoyable, enlightening, and useful. What you derived from reading this book probably depends more on where you were when you started than on any other factor. If you were already a seasoned puzzle-solver, chances are you found much of it familiar, although you may not have been clearly aware of the seven logical tactics we've explored.

On the other hand, if you were suffering from a severe case of logicophobia—and you're still reading this—you probably gained some ground but you feel the need for more practice and skill building. It would not be reasonable to expect to transform your skills completely as a result of a few hours' work; this can only be a start. If, indeed, you were in the category of extreme logicophobia, you would probably profit enormously by going into a good bookstore and buying one of the many books of thinking puzzles available, and working out every one of them with a pen and paper. If you do this, just make sure you get a book of easy puzzles, suited to your learning process. You don't want to get overwhelmed and discouraged by trying to attack the kinds of puzzles that are the favorite of the confirmed puzzle nut. There is no profit in that for you. Stick to the ones you can solve, and use them for skill building.

It is more likely, however, that you fall somewhere in between thelogicophobe and the logicophile. If you're like the majority of people, you can handle logical problem-solving processes to some extent, but you would like to get a better grip on the approaches. If you are in this category, then I hope the book has helped you to clarify what the logical mind—your mind—does when it operates in a disciplined, effective way. I also hope it has given you some useful labels to use in describing the thought process of logical reasoning.

The labels are extremely important and useful. It is not essential that you refer to the seven logical tactics by the exact same labels I have applied, but it will be very helpful if you memorize them as tactics. You need to be able to call them to mind in various situations, and to apply them when appropriate. Please take the time right now to review and memorize the seven key tactics of logical thought. They are as follows.

1. Stepping
2. Picturing
3. Rephrasing
4. Fencing
5. Itemizing
6. Chaining
7. Jumping the track

Make sure you can define each of them in your own words, and give an example of how you might use it in a problem-solving situation.

Keep in mind, also, that every one of these seven logical tactics applies across a whole wide range of problems, not only to puzzle problems like those we have been using for skill building. The same reasoning process you used to figure out the identity of the three face-down cards is a process you can use to decide how to invest your money, how to change your career, or how to make a sale. By keeping alert for various problem-solving situations, and by consciously applying these logical tactics, you will be developing your brain power every day and becoming more effective at virtually everything you want to do that involves effective, organized, systematic thought.

To round out your skill-building process, here are several thinking puzzles that call upon more than one logical tactic at a time. You may find it extremely helpful to put these various techniques together and to use them in combination on various problems. Here is a chance to practice the integration process. As you attack the following puzzles, try to use as many of the logical tactics as you can.

Practice Problem 11-1 (Combination)

A certain clock takes two seconds to strike two o'clock. How long will it take to strike three o'clock? (Be careful!)

Practice Problem 11-2 (Combination)

Bob, Carol, Ted, and Alice are sitting around a table discussing their favorite sports.

   a. Bob is sitting directly across from the jogger.
   b. Carol is to the right of the racquetball player.
   c. Alice sits across from Ted.
   d. The golfer sits to the left of the tennis player.
   e. A man is sitting on Ted's right.

What sport does each of the four prefer?

Practice Problem 11-3 (Combination)

One glass is one-quarter full of wine. A second glass, of equal size, is one-half full of wine. Fill each of the glasses to the brim with water and empty them both into another container. Now fill up one of the glasses with the mixture of water and wine. What fraction of the contents of the glass now consists of wine?

Solutions to Problems

Practice Problem 11-1 (Combination)
The interval between consecutive strikes of the clock is two seconds. For two strikes, there will be two intervals, or four seconds.

Practice Problem 11-2 (Combination)
Bob plays tennis, Carol jogs, Ted plays golf, and Alice plays racquetball.

Practice Problem 11-3 (Combination)
The mixture is three-eighths wine and five-eighths water.

Made in the USA
Columbia, SC
16 May 2021